PIMP YOUR PROFILE
How to Amplify your LinkedIn Profile on your Mobile Device

PATRICK X. GALLAGHER

ISBN: 1518772250
ISBN-13: 978-1518772252
v1

DEDICATION

I would like to thank and acknowledge the following people for inspiring me to write and complete this paperback.
My immediate family - you know who you are!

And...
Brenda Bernstein
Viveka von Rosen
Kyle Affronti
David J.P. Fisher
JD Nikolesko
Jay Ashton
Matt Foley
Andrew Foote
Chris Clein
Kailey Harris
Marc Pretorius
Rob Howard
Mats Olsson
Jennifer J Newbill
Victoria Ipri
William Watson
George Harben
Patrick Tapoka
Jawaid Ali
Matt Lovelace
Klaus Hengstmann

This page intentionally left blank.

PRAISE FOR PIMP YOUR PROFILE

This book is an intensive look at all the features of the LinkedIn phone app, not just the app itself but the various apps that you can with it. The book clearly outlines how you can take control of the LinkedIn platform through your phone.

The key strategies covered are:

• Managing the LinkedIn homepage
• How to download the apps for Apple, IOS and Android
• Golden Rule When Connecting with LinkedIn Members on Mobile App
• Using the LinkedIn App for New Connection Requests
• Building your LinkedIn profile: very extensive!
• Steps to Change your Background Color, so it shows up on the Mobile App profile
• LinkedIn Groups to join
• How to upgrade to premium and the steps involved in doing this.

The books main purpose is to show you how to "pimp" your profile in 15 minutes: this involves handling email, notifications, invitations, pulse, endorsements, profile settings, and profile surfing.

Chapter 4 is very useful because it gets into the differences between using the mobile app and the LinkedIn Web. This is clearly explained in table format that shows all of the features of both. There are full explanations of each feature as well.

Chapter 5 is the Best Practices for the app that includes backing up the app,
Give LinkedIn Feedback about their App, and Editing Your LinkedIn Profile.

Chapter 6 is the Mobile Roadmap that gets into the different version that have been released, and Chapter 7 focuses in on protecting your LinkedIn network. This provides such useful information as 6 Steps in Identifying a Fake Profile that includes:

- Look at the profile and examine the photo
- Click on the LinkedIn Member's profile name
- Check the Background Info
- Report the profile to LinkedIn.com
- Close and Ignore

Overall this book covers pretty much most of the current information you need to effectively set up, create and manage your LinkedIn profile for your mobile. The book comes with large graphs, tables and plenty of links to direct you right to the specific sites that you need to handle everything.

The author is obviously an authority on the subject and gives the reader and LinkedIn users what they need to get all set up.

- Scott B. Allan, - **Amazon Reviewer**

I have read other books by the author regarding LinkedIn and snapped the chance to read his new book Pimp Your Profile: How to Amplify your LinkedIn Profile.

The book is easy to read in one go. At the beginning I thought the pace was slow and edging towards repetitiveness. However, as soon as the introduction was over Patrick started to do what is good at: explaining in detail and in simple terms how to use LinkedIn's mobile app to boost your network and increase sales.

Here's some of the cool benefits How to Pimp Your LinkedIn Profile provides:

Handy links to apps so you can get the LinkedIn app on your handset in no time.

Great statistics about people's search trends online and how they affect the way they connect on LinkedIn and, ultimately, how you can use such statistics to build more connections.

Clear instructions how to download the app whether you use Apple or Android devices. In fact, this is one of the best tips I liked about How to Pimp Your LinkedIn Profile.

The golden rule Patrick reveals that would make massive difference to any LinkedIn user.

Specific data to help see the impact of how using LinkedIn's app from your mobile would pimp your profile if you only had to spend 15 minutes of your time.

I particularly liked two parts: the section of how to spot a fake LinkedIn profile; and the links at the end of the book directing to other books on LinkedIn written by other LinkedIn authors.

- **Paul Prifti**, Publisher

I highly recommend this book as a resource for developing a polished LinkedIn profile and becoming proficient in managing the application, all of which can be done in minutes. Having had the opportunity to personally get feedback and training from Patrick Gallagher on my LinkedIn usage, his professional expertise helped me elevate my account and habits to a professional level. LinkedIn is an integral part to networking and creating your own brand, and "Pimp Your Profile" provides great insight from an industry professional. Fun read whether you are a new or experienced user.

- **Amazon Customer**

Reid Hoffman started LinkedIn by thinking about the steps we'd take in the future to communicate professionally. Now as an ever changing mobile platform, LinkedIn is required to stay relevant in the ever virtual world. While the platform is progressive, it can be time consuming to navigate effectively. This read cuts the noise and shows you the no nonsense way to stay connected.

- **Amazon Customer**

Good book, the chapter on best practices alone makes it worthwhile. Well laid out, easy to follow and understand, and loaded with links that further expand on topics the reader may want more background on.

- **Bruce Johnston**, Sales Coach & LinkedIn Specialist

No book like **Pimp Your Profile** currently exists. This information is not only important to the average user, but goes even deeper than most users care to go, revealing technical aspects of the mobile app few of us are aware of, especially in light of the fact that LinkedIn just announced Project Voyager (their new mobile app) this week! Very good job, Patrick Gallagher.

- **Victoria A. Ipri,** LinkedIn B2B Social Selling

I liked this book because there was a ton of stuff about the LinkedIn mobile app that I did not know was available I will definitely spend more time using the LinkedIn Mobile app now. I liked Chapter 4, as there are some good features disabled on the Web version of LinkedIn.com that are still working on the LinkedIn Mobile App. Check it out folks!

- **Michael Lubnani** - Amazon Reviewer

WHY I WROTE THIS BOOK

"There are no secrets to success. It is the result of preparation, hard work, and learning from failure." - *Colin Powell*

At the time of writing this book there were over **995 reviews** on Amazon.com for the LinkedIn Mobile app and the current version of the app is 3.5.4 (android version). Amazon still has the old version in their apps store...3.4.8. This is probably because Amazon Kindle runs on Amazon's proprietary version of Android.

On Google Play Store there are currently another **792,078 reviews**.

On Apple iTunes Store there are less LinkedIn Reviews - a total of **61,026 reviews**.

After reading a lot of the online reviews and survey feedback, it seems like so many LinkedIn members do not know how they can maximize their LinkedIn profile. You can do this by learning the powerful intended purpose of the **LinkedIn Mobile app**.

Read this book and you will instantly move into the TOP 5% of knowledgeable LinkedIn Mobile App users. Even so-called LinkedIn Experts do not know the power they have in their hands!

A word on experts - there are no experts on LinkedIn! It's impossible to know everything about this social media platform. LinkedIn is constantly making updates to their platform, often without telling their members!

If you got as far as here, "**looking inside**" this book on Amazon and prefer to get the paperback version you can also get the digital version for almost no additional cost. You can read eBooks without a Kindle device as well. Check it out here:

https://www.amazon.com/about

7 Ideas you will learn by reading this book

1. What LinkedIn apps you can use on your mobile device - not just the LinkedIn App!

2. What you should do in less than 15 minutes per day

3. What features are not available in the mobile version of LinkedIn.com?

4. What advice you can ignore from the gazillion of "LinkedIn experts"

5. How to minimize your time "playing" on LinkedIn Mobile App

6. Tips on How to get around Web de-features

7. A condensed resource list of Pre-Qualified LinkedIn Experts

How will this book help you?

• You will learn to not get sucked in to using the LinkedIn mobile version. I will give you 3 simple goals to achieve every week.

• Have you heard the comment that time is money? Getting back more time will help you be more successful - right?

• You will learn how I teach LinkedIn.

• You will learn from someone who has been trained by the best of the best.

• You will learn what apps I recommend to you to use.

• Inspiration to change your habits!

What's different about this book?

As far as I can tell, no one is selling an book on Amazon.com with all of this valuable information in the one book.

Granted the LinkedIn App is easy to use, but the app comes loaded with features that you may not be aware of, or use effectively.

It contains information in it that other successful LinkedIn authors might not know, or share with others.

Like - did you know that the Web development team at LinkedIn release updates on a different schedule to the Mobile development team?

It's written by someone who eats their own dog food - meaning there is nothing in here that I haven't tried and tested. I know what works and what doesn't! You should know too!

Everything LinkedIn is doing right now is aimed for the younger generation. Don't get left behind!

Let's dive right into the content now and review **Chapter 1**...

ALSO BY THE AUTHOR

LinkedIn Secrets Revealed: 10 Secrets To Unlocking Your Complete Profile on LinkedIn.com

Publishing a Book on Amazon: 7 Steps to Publishing your #1 Book on Amazon Kindle in Minutes!

Love or Hate Email...21 Rules to Change Your - I Must Check my Email Habit. Get Back to Work and Make Money Again!

Build Your Own Living Revocable Trust: A Pocket Guide to Creating a Living Revocable Trust

Spirituality in the Workplace: A Study Guide for Business Leaders

Amazon Secrets Revealed: How To Sell More Books on Amazon.com

Pimp Your Profile: How to Amplify your LinkedIn Profile on your Mobile Device (Kindle Edition)

Trapped in a Meritocracy: Cracking the Meritocracy Code - Get Paid More for Valued Performance

Email Inbox Management: How to Master Your Inbox with Etiquette

This page intentionally left blank.

TABLE OF CONTENTS

This page intentionally left blank.

ACKNOWLEDGMENTS

I would like to thank and acknowledge the following people for inspiring me to write and complete this book.
My immediate family - you know who you are!

This page intentionally left blank.

PREFACE

With 400+* million LinkedIn Members, this social media platform - **LinkedIn.com** is a serious social media platform for business professionals. With that large membership about 10% of the LinkedIn Members are inactive. This means that the user has an account, but does not use LinkedIn. Typically, the account has been abandoned, or the member has forgotten their password.

Then there are another 20-30% that might be mobile LinkedIn Members. They will typically use their Web-browser version to setup their **100% complete profile** and then view and work with it on a mobile device.

I started using the web version of LinkedIn back in 2007, but it was not until late 2013 that I began to "play" with the mobile version of LinkedIn. Today I am using it more and more to engage with my network and Pimp My LinkedIn Profile, by liking, commenting, sharing and posting information via the LinkedIn Mobile app.

The mobile version of LinkedIn is sleek, good to look at and can help you get your social fix within a few minutes. This is one of the benefits of using the mobile version, as compared to the web version. The mobile app has several features removed to make it faster to use.

The assumption is that the user base will be mobile and will be using a variety of wireless connectivity - like 3G/4G, or WiFi to connect.

This method of connectivity is typically much slower than the wired internet.

Now... LinkedIn, of course, is giving its LinkedIn Members some free tools that come with the basic account. Some...of which I will reference in this short book. On the web version, it's called: **Who's viewed your LinkedIn profile?**

When you click on Who's viewed your LinkedIn profile on your Smart Phone/device the feature to see where your viewers come from was not available - until September 2015. Look at the image below/coming up, to see what I am referring to.

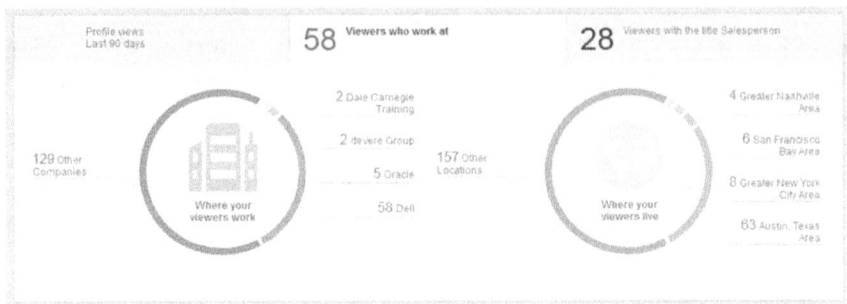

On the web version you can see right next to the Profile tab another tab called, XXX Viewers found you from LinkedIn Inbox (xxx - is the number LinkedIn shows you). Underneath that tab it shows you the number of LinkedIn members who found you from their LinkedIn Mobile app.

This means they found your profile via a LinkedIn App for iOS or Android. Edit: This was removed recently (as from 7/29/15) and then added back with certain mobile OS versions!

If I divide the total number of LinkedIn Mobile app views by my total number of views it works out to be roughly 38%. With a sum of all profile views, 38% of my profile views are from LinkedIn Mobile App members. It won't be long before this percentage will be closer to 50%.

More and more younger people are joining LinkedIn and they are used to doing much of their business and personal activity on mobile devices.

Hence the reason for this book. You should consider doing more of Pimping Your Profile via the LinkedIn App.

It makes sense - the adoption of LinkedIn on Mobile devices is growing very rapidly - I promise I will make this book short, so you can pimp your profile in 15 minutes or less.

This screen-shot currently appears on the LinkedIn App Android version 3.5.4 and the Android OS version 5 (aka: Lollipop). Strangely, it does not appear on the same apk version, but different Android kernel, like 2.3 (Gingerbread).

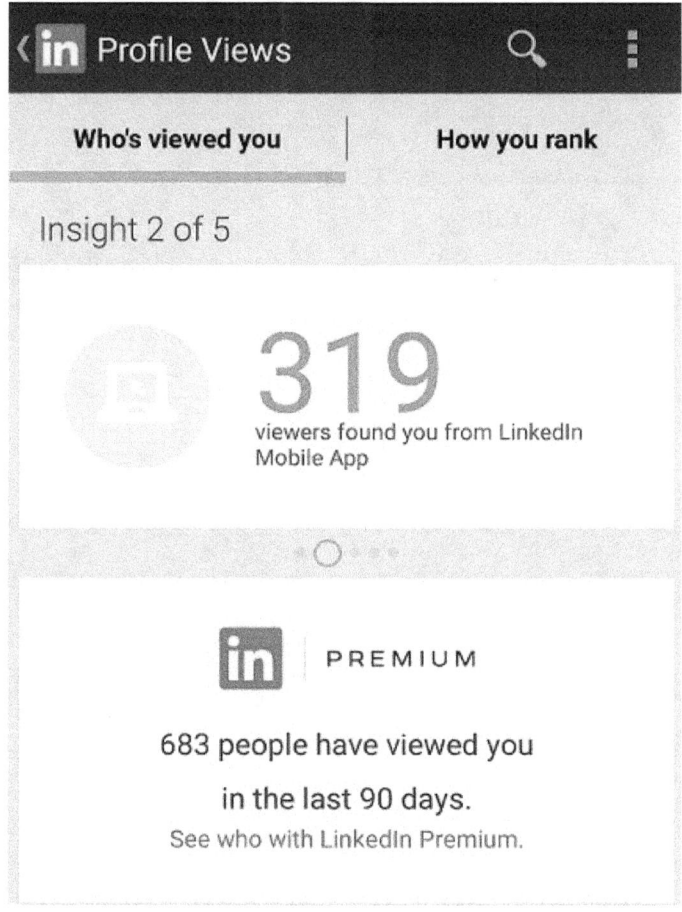

*LinkedIn Q3 2015 Earnings.

INTRODUCTION

"You have to be constantly reinventing yourself and investing in the future." - *Reid Hoffman*

When I wrote my first eBook, "**LinkedIn Secrets Revealed...**" it was an instant Sales success. It was in the Top Ten eBooks downloaded on Amazon.com for months in its browse category.

Back then in 2012, I knew very little about the publishing industry let alone the digital publishing revolution.

Since 2012, I have gradually increased my adoption rate of the mobile apps for iOS or Android. For clarification, this app was first tested on Android and the validation completed on a Samsung Mobile device. For Apple Fans, it also works there too!

You can get either OS version of the LinkedIn Mobile app here: http://www.linkedin.com/mobile

Other places to get LinkedIn Mobile app are: **Google Play, Apple App Store**, and **Amazon App Store**.

On the LinkedIn, mobile website above you will see that the mobile app is available for several phone operating systems, including: Apple, Microsoft, Google, and Blackberry.

When you get further in to reading this book you will get a full list of features that are available on the Mobile version of LinkedIn and what's on the Mobile App version.

One thing I like out of several features of the Mobile Application version is that when LinkedIn rolls out a new feature, or they disable a feature it often takes weeks and months before it gets added or removed from the mobile version. Sometimes it never gets added to the mobile app!

This is typically because the Web and Mobile development teams have different roadmaps. Roadmaps are a way of explaining the release date of a software release. See Chapter 6 for more information on roadmaps.

If a feature is not on the mobile roadmap, then that means there is no plan to add the feature. Unless you work for LinkedIn.com, you are unlikely to see what is on either Web, or Mobile Roadmap.

How much time do you have to troll through all the forums on the LinkedIn Mobile app, for example, reading all the reviews on Amazon.com? Wouldn't it be great if you could read a short book that explains to you what works and what doesn't? Even better you can carry it in your pocket and refer to it whenever and wherever - you know, like on your Smartphone.

In this book I will explain what works on the Mobile App and tell you exactly what you should do in the 15 minutes you look at LinkedIn each day. Perhaps you may increase that time on the weekends to catch up on some reading, or reconnect with your LinkedIn online network. You might also want to add some of your offline networks to the conversations.

You can learn a lot from your LinkedIn network. If you are not a LinkedIn Mobile user - you should download the app today. Download it from your preferred App store. Whatever mobile vendor you prefer just install it and try it out asap.

If you prefer to see all versions of the LinkedIn app - go here: http://www.linkedin.com/mobile

Once you have downloaded and installed your LinkedIn app for your preferred platform, let's get started straight away.

Let's keep reading together...Let's get straight to it in Chapter 1.

CHAPTER 1 - LINKEDIN MOBILE APPS

"...The Objective is not to make your links appear natural; The Objective is that your links are natural." - *Matt Cutts*

Mobile browsing is increasing every minute, every day, every week and every month. Same goes for mobile app usage. Check-out this latest usage graph from earlier this year. LinkedIn needs to improve in this environment, as there is only one subscription you can actually buy from your mobile device.

Soon more and more application developers will be tasked with adding that cart button to their application.

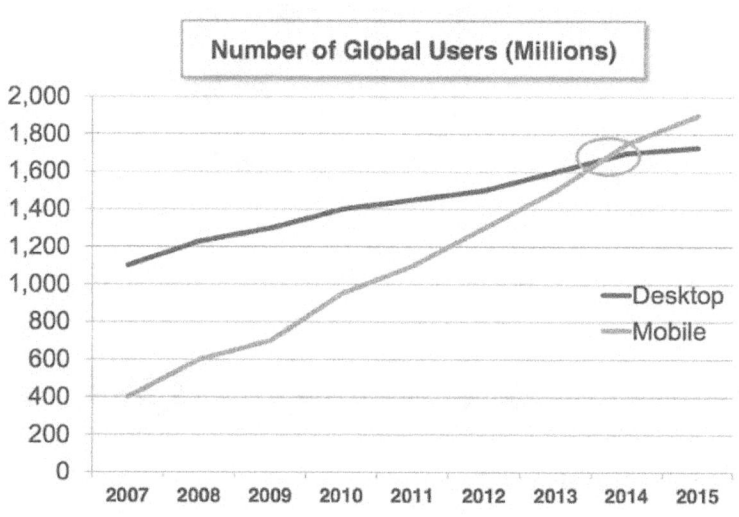

comSCORE. ©comScore, Inc. Proprietary and Confidential   24   Source: Morgan Stanley Research

According to a recent financial statement by LinkedIn, the fastest growing demographic of 39 million people are - graduates, aka millennial.

Also in LinkedIn's quarterly report they announced "Achieved its mobile moment, with the number of unique visiting members accessing LinkedIn via mobile devices **surpassing 50%. LinkedIn** continues to rapidly innovate in mobile, launching the LinkedIn Job Search app for Android during the quarter."

Source:
http://investors.linkedin.com/releasedetail.cfm?ReleaseID=909997

Guess what....? The college crowd all use a mobile device to access and engage on LinkedIn.com.

The fastest growing
demographic on LinkedIn
is the college crowd at
39,000,000

The LinkedIn Home Page

Do you use the LinkedIn Mobile app? Before you can get to your LinkedIn home page, you need to make sure you download the latest version of the app and install it on your mobile device.

One thing I like about the homepage of the LinkedIn Mobile app - is that it does not have that Facebook like view that the LinkedIn.com web version has! I don't think this feature will be rolled out in the future - either. That's just my 2 cents/pence!

What Mobile Apps?

You can download the LinkedIn Mobile app from a variety of sources. Popular sources include: ITunes store, Google Play store and Amazon Store.

Go to the back of the book for the links where you can download the apps from. Here is one you can refer to right now:

http://www.linkedin.com/mobile

There are other websites you can download the apps from too. What I recommend you do is stick to the official stores, as some websites can manipulate the apk/app to install some Trojan or other back-door hack.

There is a link to each of the official stores for you to download the LinkedIn App if you don't already have the application installed on your mobile device.

See below for version and access to the mobile versions.

World Ranking	LinkedIn Version	Release Date	Mobile Device
1	8.8.3	Sep 20th, 2015	Iphone
2	3.5.4	Oct 23rd, 2015	Android
3	8.8.3	Sep 20th, 2015	Ipad
4	10.1.31.322	Jan 27th, 2015	Blackberry
5	**Not Listed**	**Not Listed**	Windows

Apple Itunes - http://apple.co/1ekWdJg (Latest IOS app version is 8.8.3).

Google Play Store - http://bit.ly/1Ltto8f (Latest Android app version is 3.5.4). Amazon Store - I will give you two links here. I have listed them on the next page.

Direct Link to the LinkedIn App - http://amzn.to/1F6mKAy
Keep in mind that Amazon store may not have the latest version!

Here is a link to the Amazon Store App for Android -

http://amzn.to/1ApiaRb

This is the URL to install the Amazon Store App onto your Android device. The *LinkedIn App for Amazon Kindle is version 3.4.8.

There are some other LinkedIn apps that you can download as well. I won't go into too much detail as this book is mostly about the LinkedIn App.

For your convenience I will list the IOS apps first, then the Android apps. You should notice that iOS has more LinkedIn apps.

The reason is that 70% of mobile users use the iOS (Apple devices). This is because Apple has most of the market share on Smart mobile devices.

The other 30% is made up of other manufacturer mobile devices. Apple is the clear winner here. Below is an example of Smartphone OEMs just in the US. What's different about this metric is that it's only based on US users.

See next page for the graphic.

*Note: The **Amazon Kindle LinkedIn App** is not the latest version

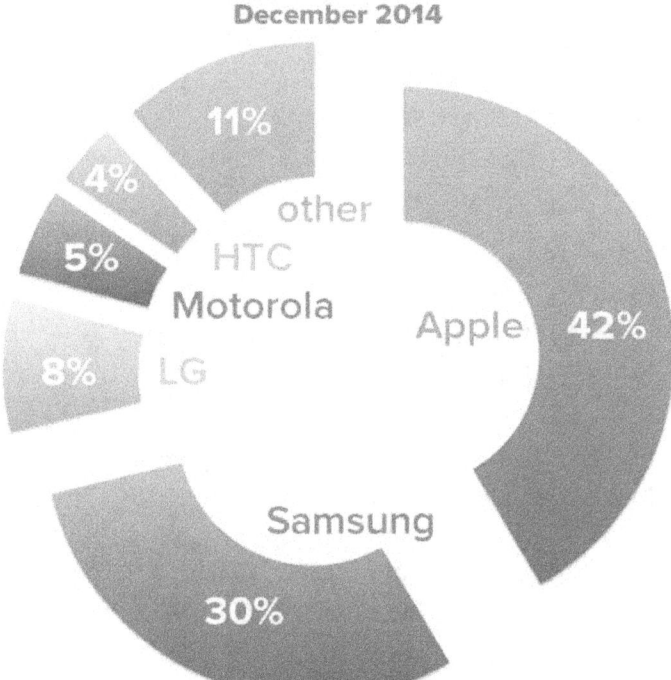

Top smartphone OEMs
among U.S. users
December 2014

11%

4%

5%

8%

other
HTC
Motorola
LG

Apple 42%

Samsung

30%

Source: comScore MobiLens, December 2014
http://www.comscore.com/Insights/Market-Rankings/
comScore-Reports-December-2014-US-Smartphone-Subscriber-Market-Share

Links to all currently supported mobile applications are below.

IOS Apps

- LinkedIn (available on Ipad) - http://apple.co/1Q1FdTP
- LinkedIn Pulse (available on Ipad) - http://apple.co/1Gukh7o
- LinkedIn Connected - http://apple.co/1cShQj4
- LinkedIn Job Search - http://apple.co/1FIvGS5
- LinkedIn Slideshare -Share Presentations (available on Ipad) - http://apple.co/1Ak09nr
- LinkedIn Recruiter - http://apple.co/1PBlyPG

IOS Apps (Cont.)

- LinkedIn Sales Navigator - http://apple.co/1el6yF3
- LinkedIn Elevate (available on Ipad) - http://apple.co/1Q1FZAl
- LinkedIn Lookup - http://apple.co/1K6Qdk2
- LinkedIn Groups - http://apple.co/1jHKNSe

Android Apps

- LinkedIn - http://bit.ly/1Ltto8f
- LinkedIn Pulse - http://bit.ly/1Apfkvw
- LinkedIn Connected - http://bit.ly/1SoJ1CJ
- LinkedIn Job Search - http://bit.ly/1F6kb1c
- LinkedIn SlideShare - http://bit.ly/1IPJ5Z6
- LinkedIn Recruiter - http://bit.ly/1FIrguz
- LinkedIn Elevate - http://bit.ly/1RakyPV

Note: The Android app doesn't have the LinkedIn Sales Navigator and also some of the newer apps do not support Android versions lower than 4.x.

The LinkedIn App for Android will work on Android OS 2.3 or newer.

Here is a screenshot of the android app store for LinkedIn app.

Protection of Your Assets

There are some BlackBerry specific apps as well. Here is a list of them…haha!! As you can see on the next page, it's a big list!!!

BlackBerry Apps

LinkedIn - Link: http://blck.by/1BgVa1L

Windows Phone App

LinkedIn - Short Link: http://bit.ly/1Ft2Uld

Both the Windows Phone OS and BlackBerry OS only have one application - only The LinkedIn App!

With that mobile app software release roadmap alone it's easy to tell who is top of the league when it comes to Primary Mobile OS App development. The Windows Phone app has not been updated since 2013!

If there was a league table for LinkedIn App software releases by mobile OS, it could look something like this...

World League Table for Mobile Devices Accessing LinkedIn (based on LinkedIn Roadmap)

World Ranking	Mobile Device
Number One!	IPhone
Number Two	Android
Number Three	Ipad
Number Four	BlackBerry
Number Five	Windows Phone

If you prefer, you can download any mobile device app version from here: http://www.linkedin.com/mobile

You can find the version you have loaded by getting to the settings button, then under "About" there will be the Version of the application installed.

For Android, this is how you can check the version. See next page.

Steps to Check apk version (for Android)*

1) Tap Settings
2) Tap Applications
3) Tap Manage Applications
4) Under Third-Party Apps, scroll to LinkedIn (usually sorted alphabetically)
5) Tap LinkedIn App Icon - right at the top it will show the version, like below

The graphic on the following page shows version 3.4.9.

LinkedIn App Version

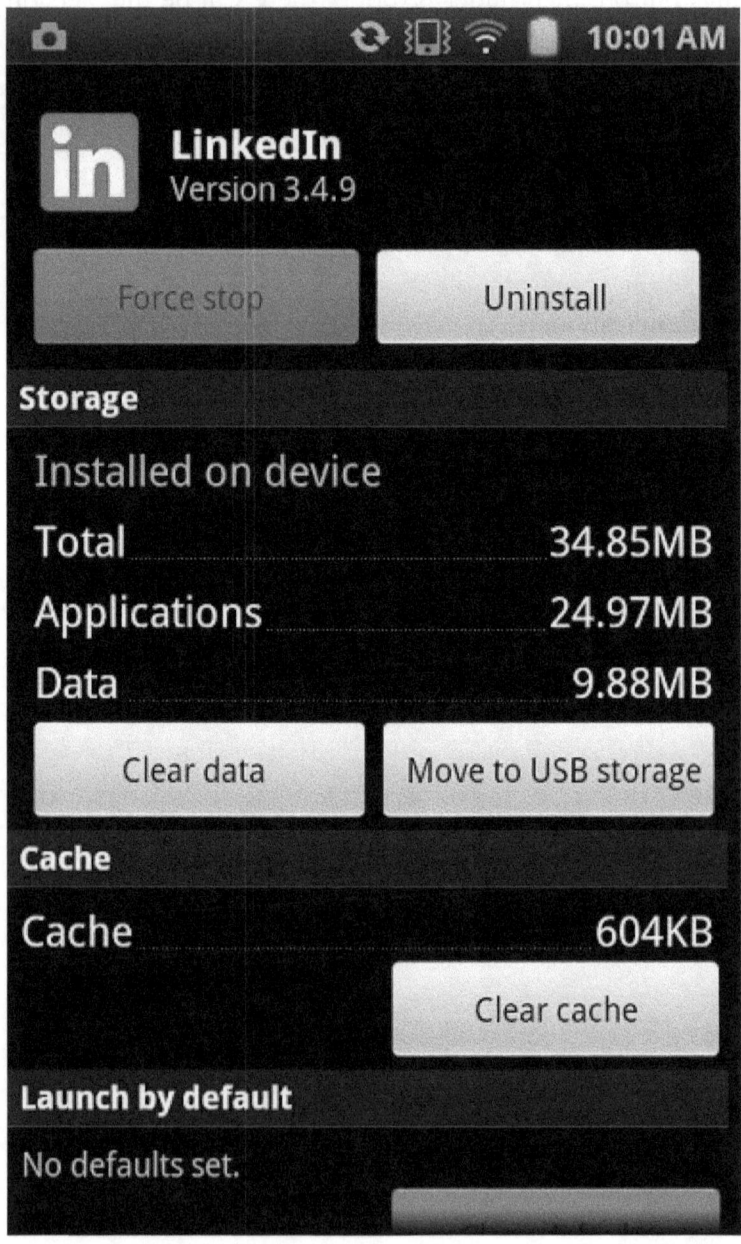

*Keep in mind that these steps to check your mobile LinkedIn app version may differ slightly by OS version and OS developer (**Google/Apple/Microsoft/BlackBerry**).

Golden Rule When Connecting with LinkedIn Members on Mobile App

About the time that the 3.4.6 version of the LinkedIn Mobile app for Android came out, the LinkedIn Mobile developer team added the ability to **customize the invite** being sent to a LinkedIn Member.

The current version of the LinkedIn Android app/apk at the time of writing this book was 3.5.4. Here is a quick link to see the table of app versions by Mobile OS.

However, on some versions of Android OS it didn't get implemented correctly. I had to log a trouble ticket as LinkedIn Members could write a customized message, but not send the message!

After taking the time to complete the customized message you could not send it!

Happily the LinkedIn App Developer team fixed it in their next release of the Android app/apk. I logged a trouble-ticket and they fixed it, along with other issues too!

Using the LinkedIn App for New Connection Requests

LinkedIn were part of the I DO NOT KNOW YOU problem because members were typically clicking/tapping that IDK button when they got connection requests that used the boiler plate connection request.

As I said earlier, now you can customize your invite.

You can create your own personal dictionary/library of standardized responses and then create a shortcut. You can find out more here: http://linkd.in/1FIkpkK

Golden Rule

99% of the time you should customize your invite. There may be occasions when you wish to just click the connect button, but that strategy should only be used 1% of your time.

Remember to practice that LinkedIn Connection request rule whenever you can.

Free Mobile Apps

Keep in mind that the software development that went into producing the application requires a lot of work by the LinkedIn Team.

For that reason, a lot of data is collected from your mobile device. See image on the next page.

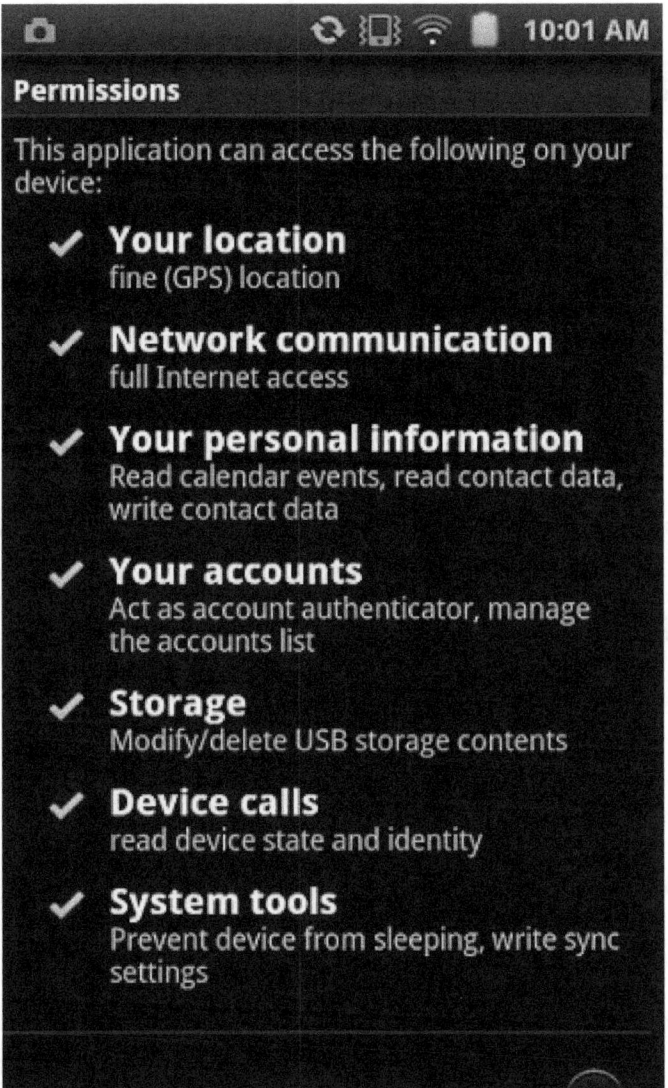

Permissions

This application can access the following on your device:

✔ **Your location**
fine (GPS) location

✔ **Network communication**
full Internet access

✔ **Your personal information**
Read calendar events, read contact data, write contact data

✔ **Your accounts**
Act as account authenticator, manage the accounts list

✔ **Storage**
Modify/delete USB storage contents

✔ **Device calls**
read device state and identity

✔ **System tools**
Prevent device from sleeping, write sync settings

There is actually more than just that one screenshot of those settings, which you give LinkedIn access to when you install the LinkedIn App. On the following page is a text summary of those settings.

LinkedIn Permissions: You automatically agree to by installing the App on your Mobile Device. This is what you agree to when installing the Mobile application.

Your Location - stores your GPS Location

Your Personal Information - Read calendar events, read contact data, write contact data

Network Communication - Full Internet Access

Your Accounts - Act as account authenticator, manage the accounts list

Storage - Modify/delete USB storage contents

Device Calls -read device state and identify

System Tools - Prevent Device from sleeping, write sync settings

Network Communication - receive data from Internet, view network state

Hardware controls - control vibrator

System Tools - read sync settings, read sync statistics, send sticky broadcast

Your accounts - discover known accounts

The LinkedIn App User Interface

Under the 3 icons you will see your page "**Home**." this links you to the daily view of your network. You can tap that and it will take you to a view of what your network is talking about.

At the top of your screen, you can see the "In" back button (top left) and to the right of it the magnifying glass and a comment icon. If you tap the icon, you can share an update.

This is the same as what you can do with your web version of LinkedIn.com. Within Network status, you can type a network status description, add an attachment from your mobile device and choose who to share with.

Your choices are usually: Public, Public+Twitter and lastly, connections. In the top right-hand corner, there is a little icon that looks like a kite (flying in the right hand direction).

Tap the kite to post your network status message. See screenshot 1 below.

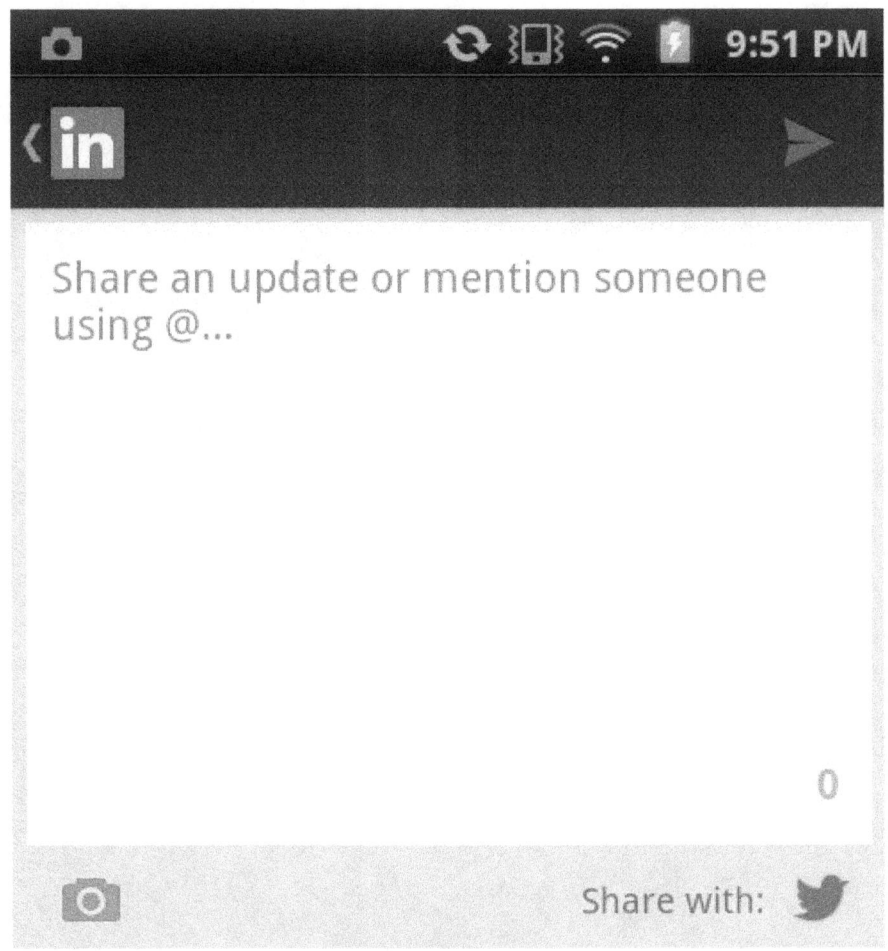

Screenshot 1

CHAPTER 2 - STARTING FROM THE TOP

*"A dream doesn't become reality through magic; it takes sweat, determination and hard work - **Colin Powell***

Your LinkedIn Homepage

The first thing you will see is your LinkedIn Homepage. Something like this...keep in mind that there are differences between all OS versions and even LinkedIn app versions!

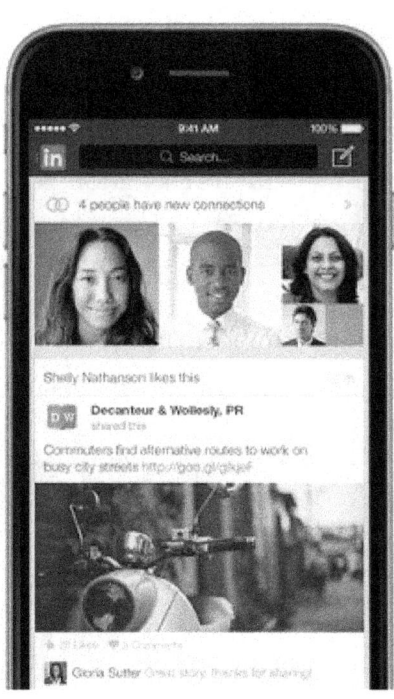

It's different as compared to the web-design. I personally prefer the app homepage over the web page. I spend more time on the mobile platform for that reason. The home page you see on the web version is like Facebook.

The LinkedIn app still has the original design interface that the web version use to have. Maybe they will change the Mobile app home page later...

LinkedIn made an announcement in October that they would b changing it!

Your LinkedIn Profile

Your LinkedIn profile picture should be next. This is a link to your LinkedIn Profile in the Mobile app. It will show your photo, along with your name, and professional headline.

Tap your headshot photo and your photo will expand - in a good way, but only if your Web photo uses the maximum pixel size recommended by LinkedIn. Tap the next section - this is your profile and will then be displayed. You will get the mobile optimized version of your profile. This means that lots of sections will need double taps to see more text in each section.

Notice under the top "In" back button you will have your name and a colored background. According to LinkedIn, this colored background is set from the Web app. A new feature was added back in 2014 that allowed premium LinkedIn members to add an avatar. You could choose the default background and upload a beautiful backdrop graphics/photo, or just go with changing the color.

Here is how you change the color on LinkedIn.com. I suggest you choose a color that resonates with you or the team you support.

Steps to Change your Background Color, so it shows up on the Mobile App profile.

1. Login to LinkedIn.com from your Personal computer (PC)
2. Scroll over to Profile and click Edit Profile
3. Move the mouse cursor away from your headshot/profile photo and in the middle you should see Edit Background (under the menu item: Interests)
4. Click on Edit Background
5. Click on Change Image
6. Change Image etc. and save

You just learned a little secret about changing the background shown on your mobile device via the LinkedIn web version. This change will only show up on the mobile app version of LinkedIn.com.

If you do not see these options it is likely you have already changed your background image color. For more information click this LinkedIn Help link: http://linkd.in/1AejUsY

In 2014 LinkedIn for Mobile added the ability to take a "Selfie."

Next to your headshot photo there is a little camera icon. When you tap your headshot you are presented with the following options: View Photo, Take a Photo and Choose a Photo.

If you choose, "Take a Photo" your camera app will load and you will get the opportunity to take a picture of something. Preferably you!

I would not recommend you take a headshot photo of yourself using this feature.

The reason I suggest this is because the photo will only be good as your camera pixel spec and you will not be able to get a professional headshot with the specification of most mobile devices' camera lens.

In my book, LinkedIn Secrets Revealed... I explain the importance of creating a professional headshot photo of yourself for your LinkedIn profile. Refer to Chapter 3 in that book.

To the right of your headshot photo you can click the "+" button if applicable.

Underneath your headshot photograph there will be your current job with brief summary of your job title captured.

Then at the bottom of the display there will be the feature to Edit Profile. I recommend you only use this feature on your mobile device if you have a full-size keyboard connected.

If not edit your profile on your PC instead. I will go through what you can change here anyhow.

To the right of your headshot photo, you can tap your headline description. You can change the following items.

1. First and Last Name
2. Region (e.g. Zip or Postal code)
3. Industry - this will bring up a long list of industries for you to scroll through!
4. Headline

I would not make any changes on your mobile device. Instead, only make changes if you find a typo or spelling mistake.

Under Experience, you can add a new job. Scroll down further and you can add a new school. Then....

- Current skills & expertise
- Summary
- Websites
- Contact Information

In Contact Information, you can update your phone number, IM contact and address.

You can scroll past the Edit profile button. You will be able to see...

- LinkedIn Publisher Posts

- Recent Activity

- Background

- Experience

- Skills & Endorsements

- Additional Info

- Personal Details

- Advice for Contacting You

- Websites

- Publications

- Projects

- Recommendations

- Volunteer & Causes

- Opportunities you are looking for

- Organizations you support

- Honors & awards

- Additional honors & Awards

- Certifications

- Education

- Organizations

- Additional Organizations

- Courses

- People also viewed

- Contact Info

- Connections

Keep in mind that if you have re-arranged your profile these headings may appear in a different order. Also, you may not have some of them on your profile, for example, if you have not filled in the publication section you won't have this listed on your LinkedIn profile.

LinkedIn Groups

If you belong to any LinkedIn groups, these will be listed under this section. You get to this section by tapping under your LinkedIn profile photo. Groups that require a moderator to allow you to join are indicated by a padlock.

These are referred to as "private" groups. At the top you will see a blue button - "Join new groups."

When you tap the blue button a list of groups will be suggested - Groups you may like. You can join one by tapping the "+" sign to the right of the group name.

Next to your name, when viewing LinkedIn groups, you can choose to go back, or search within groups. If you want to search just tap the magnifying glass and the group search will be automatically be selected. Type your search keywords in the search button, as below, or on the next page.

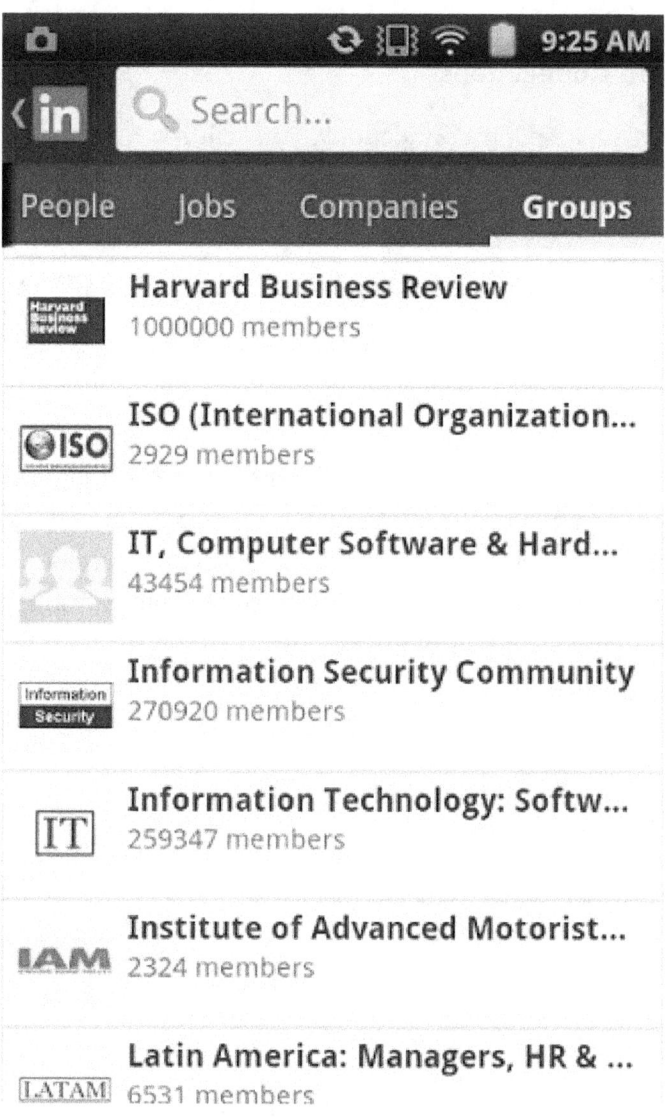

Screenshot2

When you tap a group it will show - Popular discussions. You can tap the person's name who is leading the discussion, click within the discussion to load external content, or leave a comment on the Group post, or click the like button on the group post.

For the last 2 activities, this will show up on your LinkedIn activity page.

LinkedIn Connections

When you tap on connections, you will see a list of your current LinkedIn Members connected to you. You can view your connections by tapping on a name.

At the top you will see, "People You May Know." You can click on the photos and the **"People You May Know"** link will be activated. Click on the back button within Connections and you have two remaining options.

You can click on the magnifying glass, or the +People Icon. The +People Icon will take a look at your personal address book and send connection requests (after asking for permission) to those connections it finds email addresses for. I typically skip this way of expanding my LinkedIn network.

When you tap on the magnifying glass it will bring up the "People" Search window. You can type in keywords to find a keyword specific LinkedIn profile.

Note: In 2015 with the *Free* LinkedIn membership (most members have), the company introduced the feature whereby you can only search for people up to 100 times per month. Once you have reached that limit you have to wait until the next month. Otherwise your people searches are limited and do not reset to zero until the month has completed. **However, this feature limitation is not in place on LinkedIn for Mobile.**

LinkedIn Companies

When you tap on this shortcut, it will bring up the list of companies you are following. You can tap on the company name and it will bring up details from the company's LinkedIn Homepage. The company home page is divided into sections as follows:

About Company Name; Jobs at Company Name; Posts at Company Name; then you will be able to tap at the bottom similar companies.

At the very top, you have the opportunity to follow new companies. When you tap that button, you will be presented with a long list of companies that are listed on LinkedIn. Looking through the list it appears that the list is sorted according to the company names I already follow.

You can follow more companies by clicking the "+" sign to the right of the company name.

Jobs

Jobs are divided into 3 sections. Jobs You've Saved; Jobs You've Applied For and Jobs Recommended for You.

If you tap within the **Jobs Recommended for You** - you can save the job. Once you have saved the job it will be added to the **Jobs You've Saved section**. You can tap back into this section and Unsave Job, or apply on the company website. I recommend you apply for any job using your PC and not your mobile device to avoid typos and spelling issues.

Tapping on the magnifying glass within the Jobs section of your mobile profile will bring up the search feature. You can switch between people, companies and groups as well. Under the Jobs tab, you have the option to type in your current location. I am not sure if this is currently working with version 3.4.6 of the Mobile app.

Pulse

This shortcut is also a separate app on Android and iOS. What is Pulse? **Pulse is the LinkedIn News app**. Your LinkedIn News provided by the Pulse App is made of the Channels you are following. I will go into more detail about the Pulse App in Chapter 3.

Other shortcuts

You can add other shortcuts to your LinkedIn Mobile App homepage. These can be: **LinkedIn Groups, People you May Know**, Who's Viewed Your Profile, Your Recent Activity and Groups You May like. To add more (assuming you have not maxed out) your shortcuts, tap the Add Shortcut button.

Upgrade to Premium

Tap this button if you want to see what the current price is for the Premium LinkedIn Subscription service.

Settings

Here you can also upgrade to the Premium subscription. In addition, you can…

-Add connections (from your phone)

-Sync LinkedIn with your phone

-Turn off/on System Notifications

-Turn off/on Push Notifications - there is a whole section of notifications to turn off if you prefer to do so

-Get Version information

-Help Center: You can search the help database

-Privacy Policy

-Device-specific EULA

-User Agreement - surprisingly this is optimized for viewing on a mobile device

-Others: Two options - Sign out & Copyright Info

This page intentionally left blank.

CHAPTER 3 - PIMP YOUR PROFILE IN 15 MINUTES

"If you plant the right seed in the right spot, it will grow without further coaxing." – **BJ Fogg**

What can you do in 15 minutes?

You will be surprised! You can do a lot in 15 minutes... At the end of these choices I will recommend what you should work on in those precious 15 minutes you have every day. Here are your choices

What is Pimp Your Profile all about? It's actually not what you are thinking....

It's not about you first and foremost, but it is about your LinkedIn Network. It's all those LinkedIn members who need their message amplified to your network for your network and theirs. Just remember - it's not directly about YOU! But it does start from you taking action. What am I talking about?

This is where you comment, share and like the publisher posts, the network shares, the photos and any other activity updates that your LinkedIn network is talking about. Your network needs your amplification. You can help.

You can spend up to 15 minutes by pimping their profile first!

When you Pimp someone else's profile, you are going to indirectly advertise who you are and what you care about. This will communicate your personal brand and values to your network. Eventually, your network will see how you help them and may appreciate you for that by returning some amplification for your posts, shares and likes.

At the top of your LinkedIn Homepage, you have email, notifications and invitations. You can start with any of those. I suggest you start moving from left to right at the top. Start with your email.

Email

If you have received new email, keep in mind you want to deal with the task of processing email immediately. Meaning if you read the email and there is no action required you should delete the email. 60% of email that is filed is never retrieved or read again.

On the mobile app, the complete message may not be displayed based on the Mobile OS you are using to access LinkedIn.com...some of the content may be truncated.

Try and be as efficient as possible. You only have 15 minutes! If you need some help with email, I suggest you read my book: **Email Inbox Management: How to Master Your Inbox with Etiquette.** Short Link: http://amzn.to/1EpQUA1

Notifications

Look at the notifications, but don't tap any of them as you will waste a lot of time for your device to be refreshed with the content that you are being notified about. Leave that for your web activity. Your mobile will have a reduced bandwidth, especially if you have a lot of apps installed on it.

Invitations

You can send out invitations, but this may take 30-60 seconds per invite, unless you prefer to just tap the bubble circle and hope! Sending a customized message takes time and you might want to leave that task for when you have a full-sized keyboard and greater bandwidth.

Pulse

Pulse can be installed as a separate app. You can configure it to show relevant news to send to your device. It's also part of the LinkedIn app. You choose whether you want to install a separate application or not. Remember each application you install on your mobile device may slow it down.

Connections

Three ways you can make connections. I suggest three ways to make connections. There are more, but let's keep it simple.

1) **PYMK** - People You May Know: Tap the shortcut on your mobile device and just click on the "+Headshot icon" It's really easy, but for some receiving the invite they may ignore your invite because you didn't make the connection message personal. Essentially you used LinkedIn's boiler plate connection invite without using the Mobile App's customized connection request

2) **Use the Search feature** - type in some keywords and then tap on the profiles that come up. You can either click on the "+headshot"

3) **Click on the Homepage** - send connection requests to LinkedIn members who have shared content you like, or comments etc. - mention it in your customized connection request

Note: Don't forget to customize your invite!

Endorsements

You will find that endorsing your LinkedIn network is much easier than it is on LinkedIn.com web version. I recommend you spend some time doing this whenever you have the chance. Schedule it in your daily 15 minutes, or just make a 1 day of the week where you click on profiles.

Find out more about endorsements. Here is a link to my LinkedIn Publisher post - https://www.linkedin.com/pulse/linkedin-endorsements-how-turn-them-off-patrick-gallagher

Profile Surfing

This is a good way to increase your profile views, by clicking on other profiles.

The best way to do this is to click on a profile from the home page where someone has posted a network update from someone in their network, but are not directly connected to you - 1st level connection. Click on a 2nd level connection.

Another way you can do this is to click on the home page, then go to "Who's Viewed Your Profile." Return their LinkedIn member's view of your profile on theirs. Return Browse for short!

If you have a Premium LinkedIn account then you will be able to return browse on more member profiles. The basic LinkedIn account will only let you return browse on 5.

Keep in mind that if you are getting a lot of daily page views you are missing out on the opportunity to return browse on profiles! Assuming you are getting more than 5 profile views (PVs) per day.

You might notice too in the acknowledgement section of this book I have mentioned all the names of the people who helped contribute. I created links to the LinkedIn Public profile. That's a great example of **Pimping Your Profile!**

LinkedIn Mobile Survey Results

In a recent survey, I was surprised how little the 350+ million based community know about the LinkedIn mobile application. For example, one LinkedIn Survey response did not know you can customize LinkedIn Invitations. This feature was added around 3.4.6 version on the android app.

LinkedIn finally realized that they were part of the problem of members clicking I do not Know (IDNK) this person.

Here is an Infographic displaying the survey results for LinkedIn Mobile use.

The survey had some interesting responses. See the next page for an InfoGraphic I have designed based on the survey data.

USING LINKEDIN
ON MOBILE DEVICES

WORLD RANKINGS
#1 IOS - #2 ANDROID - #3 IPAD

44% of Users Surveyed Use Android Devices to Browse LinkedIn

40% of Users Surveyed Use iOS Devices to Browse LinkedIn

4% of Users Surveyed Use Blackberry Devices to Browse LinkedIn

12% of Users Surveyed Use Windows Devices to Browse LinkedIn

Users surveyed spend an overall average of 13.68 minutes browsing LinkedIn with iOS Users spending the most time on average of 60 minutes.

32% of Users Surveyed Use LinkedIn to View Profiles, Email and Communicate.

28% of Users Surveyed use LinkedIn to Connect w/ Others.

72% of All Mobile Users Surveyed Recommended App Changes to LinkedIn.

With 12% being the highest for being able to see who viewed their post.

7% of Users Surveyed Made No Recommendations for Application Changes for LinkedIn Across all Mobile Platforms.

Top 3 Uses of LinkedIn

 The "Like" Feature

 Connecting With Others

 Emailing Other Connections

Summary

Not Surprisingly LinkedIn has designed their UI on the LinkedIn app in the way they feel the end user - YOU will use the app.

That means that you should spend 3 minutes per day (my recommendation) in each of these 5 areas.

In no order of priority - you can choose...

1) **Email** - check your email to see if you have email. Keep in mind that you will get a copy of the email on both the web version and the app version

2) **Notifications** - see who has accepted your invitation, published, viewed your profile, liked your update, or endorsed you for a skill

3) **Invitations** - your recent connections will be listed first. Any invitations you have viewed previously will also be listed, but you will have to tap View All Invitations

4) **Like** - from the Home page tap the "Thumbs Up" icon on an update from your network

5) **Share/Comment** - click the share icon, or comment on your network's post, network status update

My Recommendation: To **Pimp Your Profile in 15 minutes**, or less you should focus on items 4) and 5). Read this book - **Give and Take:** Why Helping Others Drives Our Success short link: http://amzn.to/1SoGvPt

If you do anything else on your mobile app you will end up taking more time than 15 minutes. Do what the experts recommend and do these tasks each day. By doing tasks 4 & 5 you will surely grow your network.

Here is a snapshot of what the experts do every day...

-Use the "Like" feature
-Connect With Others
-Read their Email

Again refer back to the Survey results to look at what other LinkedIn Members do on their LinkedIn mobile app.

CHAPTER 4 - LINKEDIN APP VERSUS LINKEDIN WEB

"We are all of us stars, and we deserve to twinkle."- *Marilyn Monroe*

What's Different?

The mobile application version of LinkedIn.com is different because of the constraints of sending information over the member's carrier network. LinkedIn.com will typically send information from the host to the client via the wired connection (CAT-5) network cable.

The Mobile app version will be sending the information over the air via a variety of network protocols that mobile devices use, such as: Wi-Fi, 2G/3G/4G etc. Each of those networks have their own set of protocols that get used to acknowledge that data got from a to b etc.

One of the major benefits of using the LinkedIn Mobile app over the web version is that no email, or dialogue box is required. This means you can literally tap one button and it will send a connection request without additional steps to be completed.

Let's see a summary of what the differences are in table format.

Here is a list of the major differences. By all means this is <u>not</u> a **complete list!** I have put them in a handy table for you to review and take notice of. This list is listed on the next page.

LinkedIn Feature	Web	Mobile	More Information
Commercial Use Limit	Yes	No	https://premium.linkedin.com/professional/faq
View Activity	Yes	Yes	Click on the Profile of a LinkedIn Member - Send InMail button
Alternative views of your updates	Yes	No	On the web version you have a button, that says: "View Profile As"
Notifications	Yes	Limited	May be Limited on Ipad
LinkedIn Feature	**Web**	**Mobile**	**More Information**
Invitations to connect	Yes	Limited	On the web version you have multiple choices of how you know the person etc.
Groups	Yes	Limited	Under Interests on LinkedIn.com. Mobile is limited to what you can do versus web
How You Rank for Profile Views	Yes	No	Under Who's Viewed your Profile on LinkedIn.com
Who's viewed your posts	Yes	No	Click Profile, then Who's Viewed your Profile on LinkedIn.com - there are stats on mobile app
LinkedIn Feature	**Web**	**Mobile**	**More Information**
Your Decision Board	Yes	No	Not sure how long this feature will last on web version
Connections: Keep in Touch	Yes	Limited	Shows people you may know and connection list
Find Alumini	Yes	No	Under Connections on LinkedIn.com
Education - All Menu Items	Yes	No	Education is between Connections and Jobs on LinkedIn
LinkedIn Feature	**Web**	**Mobile**	**More Information**
Business Services	Yes	No	This is on the top right side of the LinkedIn.com Menu
Endorsements	Yes	No	When you click on a mobile profile you are not asked to endorse them
Relationship Button in Contacts	Yes	No	Here you add reminder, notes, How you met, tag etc. Not available on mobile

LinkedIn Feature	Web	Mobile	More Information
Personal LinkedIn Avatar	Yes	No	You will see the default color you picked before personalization. Customization is not available on the mobile app
LinkedIn Profile Summary	Yes	Limited	You need to tap the summary twice to expand on mobile device. Put phone # in first paragraph
Boolean Search	Yes	Limited	You can do this on the Mobile App, but there is no advanced search feature
LinkedIn Publisher	Yes	No	You cannot create publisher articles on the mobile app. Also images and videos for published content do not show up on the mobile*

Explanations of each LinkedIn Feature

Once you have installed the app it will take around 31.38MB of space on your mobile device. In addition to that space requirement there is also space needed for the other LinkedIn applications and user data.

Version 3.5.1.2

This table was originally compiled using the android version 3.5.1.2. Keep in mind that each time a new release comes out of the app, the app footprint increases and some feature enablement may change.

That means the app will take up more memory on your mobile device. My favorite app version is 3.4.9, as it had a smaller footprint and typically takes less time to get stuff done when tapping a feature, or viewing an update from your network.

On one of my test devices for writing this book I gave up on looking at some updates, as it just took too long over wifi to deliver the content to my mobile device.

On a newer device, like an iPhone 6, or Samsung S5/S6 content delivery is faster, even over the same network connection!

Permissions

This is probably the biggest issue with some LinkedIn members not wanting to use it, or install the App.

Remember the statement - There is no such thing as a "FREE" lunch.

Well this is true in the case of the permissions of this Smart device - mobile application. In order to have this app installed for FREE on your mobile device you have to give away the following information.

-GPS Location (only if you turn on GPS)
-Your personal information (calendar events, contact data etc.)
-Network communication (full internet access)
-Your accounts (manage the accounts list)
-Storage (Modify/delete USB storage contents)
-Device Calls (read device state and identify)
-System Tools (Prevent device from sleeping, write sync settings)

If you install the Pulse App (version 4.2.2) as well, it has access to: Your Location; Storage; Network communication and System Tools.

So if you install the LinkedIn Mobile App, just keep in mind what you are sending to LinkedIn whenever you have your device turned on and are using the app. Perhaps you don't really care...

*When you publish, or view a LinkedIn publisher post on an android device (regardless of the android os version) images, or video (like YouTube), they do not show up on your mobile - android OS version 2.3.

According to LinkedIn - this is working as designed. What you get is a big white blank space where the image should be.

This was the response from LinkedIn Technical Support team member, who then closed the ticket...

LinkedIn Response 04/25/2015 07:00

Hi Patrick,

Thanks for your reply and confirmation. I see that you have few videos uploaded, however the mobile app version do not have functionality to play videos.

You may use the mobile browser full website option to view them.

Regards,

Santosh

Customer Experience Advocate

This page intentionally left blank.

CHAPTER 5 - LINKEDIN MOBILE APP BEST PRACTICES

"Books are a uniquely portable magic." - *Stephen King*

A little known opportunity

When do your LinkedIn members in your network respond to your favorite posts, comments, status on LinkedIn? You should schedule these items first thing in the morning for the time zone where most of your network resides.

Then the next largest network time zone and so forth. I always review my network, like a triangle...Americas, Europe and Asia.

When I say schedule I don't meet literally! I'm not talking about using *hootsuite*, or *bufferapp*, but rather - you actually schedule time on your calendar - up to 15 minutes to amplify your network's content. You can't schedule "Likes!"

Set deliberate intentions every day to do your amplifications! **Pimp Your Profile** via your LinkedIn network!

These intentions can be giving your network's content: the thumbs up (liking), commenting, and sharing posts on other social networks, like **Google+,** or **Twitter**.

Backup the App

On Android, use a backup application, like **MyBackup**, or **Titanium Backup**. Both of these applications are available for IOS and Android. I use the paid version of both applications. I recommend you do as well.

Before you update the LinkedIn App, make sure you back it up. In fact I recommend you do this for most of your important applications. I use my offline memory to backup the apks.

You do this in case you need to revert back to a previous version. Google keeps a backup for you as well ☺.

I have had several encounters with bad apks. When a new revision comes out - there will be several fixes in the latest revision of the application that also breaks something else. For example with **3.4.6, LinkedIn** introduced several versions on their road map that were fairly close together in their launch dates.

One time they introduced a new feature that has been around since the 3.4.x version of android that allows you to customize your invitation to connect message.

However, once you had written your invitation message, you could not actually send the message - Doh!

I logged a LinkedIn Trouble-Ticket for that. You should provide feedback too if you think something is not working as designed, or you have some suggestions on improving a feature.

Give LinkedIn Feedback about their App

When something does not work as it should, I always take the opportunity to log an issue and provide feedback. Of course, I first check with LinkedIn Help (click the Twitter Button below) to see if what I am experiencing in the app is an issue or not.

@LinkedInHelp usually responds with a message containing a link to log an issue with their technical support team. Type in this url link to bring up a conversation with the @LinkedInHelp page on Twitter. Here is the url: https://twitter.com/linkedinhelp

You can also get help from this link here, This is specifically for the mobile app: http://linkd.in/1qHaRvI

If you have a basic "free" LinkedIn account it may take some time for the team to respond, but they usually respond within a 24 hour period. Some of their technical support team members are based in India.

It helps if you include in your "Tweet" message a screen capture of the issue - assuming you use Twitter to alert them of the issue. Click the Twitter icon to see what a Tweet message looks like. You can also attach a screen-shot, like in the image below...

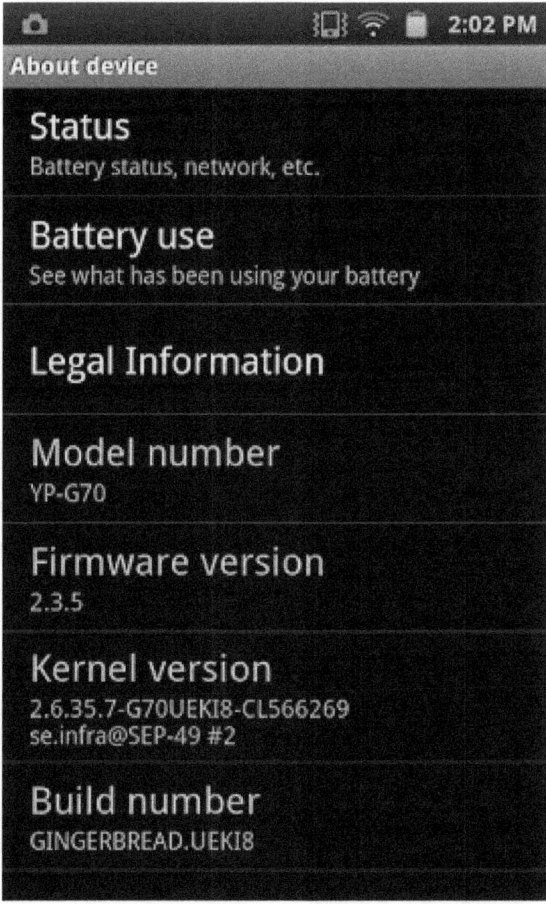

Instructions on how to attach an image to a LinkedIn trouble ticket can be found here:
https://help.linkedin.com/app/answers/detail/a_id/223

Here is a link to the LinkedIn Help Center - https://help.linkedin.com/app/ask/path you can change details once you click on the url based on your mobile device.

Editing Your LinkedIn Profile

You can edit your profile on your mobile device. I can't remember when this feature was introduced, but now you can edit your profile - just like you can on the web version. I recommend you edit your profile on the web version - typically you will have access to a full-size keyboard.

With a touch-screen on mobile devices it is too easy to insert mistakes into your profile.

What you can and should do is review your profile from your mobile. If you spot any typos, or spelling errors you can correct these on your mobile. I actually recommend all LinkedIn members view their profile on their mobile - **you will be surprised how different it looks** - even though it's the same profile!!!

Your Smart Device

A word of caution - when you install an app on your **smartphone** - you are giving away your privacy. If this is something that may concern you, then at the very least, please install this app from John McAfee. It's called **D-Vasive**. This link is to the Android version of the app. Link: http://bit.ly/1Z9BAT6

Remember nothing is FREE in life! You are paying something - what you are paying for is your loss of privacy.

If you need to ask the LinkedIn mobile team a question, here is their email address: team-mobile@linkedin.com

CHAPTER 6 - MOBILE ROADMAP

"An average person with average talent, ambition and education, can outstrip the most brilliant genius in our society, if that person has clear, focused goals." - *Brian Tracy*

Mobile Roadmap

A Roadmap as you know helps you plot a journey from A to B. A being your start point and B being your final destination.

Similarly, in software a roadmap helps the development team, in this case the LinkedIn development team - reference what they are going to deliver at a specific roadmap point.

For example if the current version of the LinkedIn Android Apk is 3.5.3, then it is logical to assume that the next version will be 3.5.4. The team will have a list of fixes and features that they will deliver at that time.

Here is a recent android apk app roadmap for LinkedIn with the version and date of delivery. Work from the left to right. The far right hand column is the latest version, at the time of writing this book.

Version	3.4.7	3.4.8	3.4.9	3.5.2	3.5.2.1	3.5.3
Date	3/9/15	4/5/15	5/1/15	5/28/15	7/24/15	09/25/15

Official LinkedIn apk page:

https://developer.linkedin.com/content/dam/developer/apk/LinkedIn-3.5.1.apk- this link is not the latest version of LinkedIn Android app.

Note: version 3.5.3 had a major revision for the new **LinkedIn Messenger** that came out previously on the web version of LinkedIn.com. If you used older apk's to access your messenger mail, once it had been transitioned to the new web version, you would get a lot of time-outs. If you are using an older app you should upgrade.

What has surprised me with LinkedIn's Software release roadmap is how disconnected, or disjointed it is. For example...the same apk version 3.5.3 has a different feature set as compared to the exact apk on another android device using an older android OS - comparing **Gingerbread** to **Lollipop**.

Here is a quick primer on the Android versions. The latest operating system version is called Android 5.0 "*Lollipop.*"

Android Name	Version
Lollipop	5.0
KitKat	4.4
Jelly Bean	4.1
Ice Cream Sandwich	4.0
Honeycomb	3.0
Gingerbread	2.3

There are other older versions, but they are really not worth talking about, or using!

For more information review the website: https://www.android.com/history/

LinkedIn App Home

Where do you get the mobile application from? You should get it from your app store. Be very careful about installing the applications outside of the application store - you might accidently install a malware script if you do not download from the official app store. Here is a list of where you should install from.

Apple Itunes - http://apple.co/1ekWdJg (Latest IOS app version is 8.6.2)

Google Play Store - http://bit.ly/1Ltto8f (Latest Android app version is 3.5.2)

Amazon Store - I will give you two links here. I have listed them below.

Direct Link to the LinkedIn App - http://amzn.to/1F6mKAy Keep in mind that Amazon store may not have the latest version!

Here is a link to the Amazon App for Android - http://amzn.to/1ApiaRb

This is the url to install the Amazon Store App onto your android device.

BlackBerry Apps

LinkedIn - Link: http://blck.by/1BgVa1L

Windows Phone App

LinkedIn - Short Link: http://bit.ly/1Ft2Uld

This page intentionally left blank.

CHAPTER 7 - PROTECTING YOUR LINKEDIN NETWORK

*"As the Internet of things advances, the very notion of a clear dividing line between reality and virtual reality becomes blurred, sometimes in creative ways." - **Geoff Mulgan***

Do you ever think of your LinkedIn network as an asset?

If you don't, some surely do. That's why they create fake LinkedIn profiles, to get the email addresses and other information of your high-value, authoritative network.

You engage on LinkedIn; connect with members and potential customers, participate in group discussions and publish your own content through LinkedIn's Publishing Platform. All of this takes time.

Getting your high-value connections to 500+ is a meticulous process. So, while you use LinkedIn innocently, accepting most requests for connecting, fake LinkedIn members opportunistically lurk.

They want to connect — not because they want to do business with you — but because you are the window to a priceless pool of lead information.

You can identify fake LinkedIn profiles and make it a safer platform for you and your network.

How do You Spot a Fake LinkedIn Profile?

It's easy to spot fraudulent LinkedIn profiles that try to gain access to your network and then download the email addresses of your connections.

After a while of following this process you won't even have to follow all these steps, it will become an automatic process, one that protects your network and ensures LinkedIn remains a safe platform for the exchange of ideas and the discovery of talent.

6 Steps in Identifying a Fake Profile

1) When you get a LinkedIn Connection request from someone, always login to LinkedIn.com before clicking on the accept button in your inbox.

Why?

People with fake email connection requests might attempt to snag your login credentials by sending you a fake connection request. The connection request will take you to a fake webserver to capture your email and password. Yikes.

2) Once on LinkedIn.com, look at the profile and examine the photo (assuming there is one). If you are using Chrome you can install an extension called: TinEye Reverse Image Search. Short link:

https://www.tineye.com/

This tool helps you find other versions of the same image. It will tell you quickly - if the name does not match the photo and/or profile. Here are two examples of fake profiles that tried to connect with me recently.

See next page for example images of Fake LinkedIn member accounts trying to connect with me.

Why are these fake?

In the first photo, something did not quite add up. I instantly felt there was a conspicuous mismatch between the woman's name and her job location.

Let me explain. Common sense tells me that if you work for a French company in France, it's highly likely that you're French too. In this case, the name is English not French.

I ran her image through **TinEye** and confirmed by hypothesis, that Amelia's profile is fake and that her attempt to connect with me was solely based on malicious intentions.

For Mollie's profile, my intuition instantly flagged this as a spammer. I didn't even have to run this picture through **TinEye** to know it's a stock photo.

Just to be 100% sure though I did go through the next steps in my fake LinkedIn profile identification process.

3) Click on the LinkedIn Member's profile name (not the "x" or "tick" mark). You should now be viewing the suspicious LinkedIn profile.

Scroll down to that person's Connections. On the top right of that box click on Shared. This will display all LinkedIn members you have in common.

You might think, "If others have connected with this person, then this wouldn't be a spammer, would it?"

Wrong. Some people want so badly to get 500+ connections they aren't as selective as to who they're connecting with. Don't be that person. Don't compromise yourself and your network's value.

Even if you share a few connections, don't accept their invitation just yet. (Unless some people in your network know or have talked to this person).

4) Check the Background Info - Typically, a spammer doesn't have a complete profile. More often than not, their education and current position do not make sense either.

In Mollie's case, she has given herself away, Hogwarts (sadly) only exists in Harry Potter. Gotcha! More often than not a fake profile is sparsely populated, there won't be much information filled in. Why? It takes too much time, which the owner of the fake profile isn't interested to spend on it.

5) **Report the profile to LinkedIn.com** - before you click on that "x" be responsible and report this fake LinkedIn profile to LinkedIn.com.

Here is how you do it - At the top of the spammer's profile click the Down arrow as seen below. Then click on "**Block or Report**."

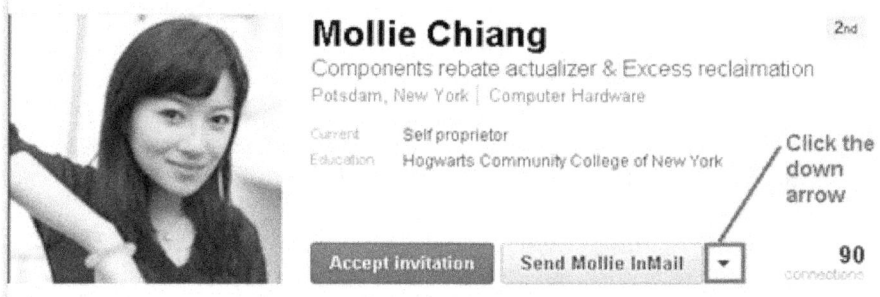

Click on the Report box, then in the dropdown menu choose Flag Profile as Misrepresentation. In the details box you can be more specific: Fake LinkedIn Profile.

Click on the Agree button to report the profile to LinkedIn.com.

6) Close and Ignore. Now go back to your Add Connections Icon (represented by grey headshot with a + sign) and click the ignore sign.

You can go a step further and click the "I don't know this person (aka IDK). Note that this link disappears if you click away after clicking the "x."

If you prefer to skip all that you can simply click the "x" button.

LinkedIn: A safe, professional business network

When we ignore fake LinkedIn profiles we contribute to the turning of LinkedIn into a Fake Profile Heaven. Act responsibly, protect yourself and your network by consciously choosing who to connect with and who to ignore or report. Before I even finished writing this chapter, several more LinkedIn connection requests came in. All fake.

Please do your bit and report fake profiles to LinkedIn.com so that it becomes the digital hub of idea exchange and talent discovery it was destined to be.

Note: This activity needs to be executed from the web version of LinkedIn.com.

Fake Profile Links: "Amelia" and "Mollie" are below.

Amelia: http://linkd.in/1DI43pp

Mollie: http://linkd.in/1OeKczQ

ABOUT THE AUTHOR

Patrick Gallagher provides his talent & services to a major Fortune 50 company.

Everything that is shared with you in this book is shared to help you spend more quality time with your friends and family. When Patrick is not at work he enjoys spending time in his garden and playing tennis with his family, or friends.

Patrick is active in community affairs and regularly volunteers for local charities in Texas. Patrick enjoys spending as much time as possible with his family. He currently lives and works in sunny and very hot, Texas. In Texas there are only two seasons: Warm season and hot season!

Patrick can be reached at (424) 703-GOAL, or Click on his LinkedIn Profile, You can also connect with him on his Twitter page.

Short Link: http://linkd.in/PLLBUf

This page intentionally left blank.

SOURCES - FURTHER READING - BOOKS FOR REFERENCE

I put this list together based on current sales of similar book titles. These are the books that Amazon is telling me that are currently selling very well. The top 20! Keep in mind with the "Internet of Things." this top 20 list may have changed by the time you read this book!!!

1) **LinkedIn: The Top Job Hunting Tips And Tricks** (And Mistakes to Avoid) When Creating a LinkedIn Profile (Job hunting, career search, LinkedIn, job change, ... hunting online, LinkedIn profile Book

2) **LinkedIn: Tell Your Story, Land The Job**

3**) How to Use LinkedIn to Sell More Books** (Writer's Platform Book 2)

4) **How to Write a KILLER LinkedIn Profile**... And 18 Mistakes to Avoid: 2015 Edition (11th Edition)

5) **LinkedIn: Guide To Making Your LinkedIn Profile Awesome**: 25 Powerful Hacks For Your LinkedIn Profile To Attract Recruiters and Employers (Career Search, ... profile, LinkedIn makeover, career search)

6) **LinkedIn Riches: How to Leverage the World's Largest** Professional Network to Enhance Your Brand, Generate Leads and Increase Revenue!

7) **Go From Zero to Hero on LinkedIn**: Jump Start your Prospecting Success in as Little as 7 Days

8) **Connect: The Secret LinkedIn Playbook To Generate Leads**, Build Relationships, And Dramatically Increase Your Sales

9) **LinkedIn: LinkedIn for Business: 25 Hacks & Tips** to grow your Network and Generate Leads for your Business with LinkedIn

(LinkedIn, LinkedIn for business, social media)

10) **LinkedIn In 30 Minutes:** How to create a rock-solid LinkedIn profile and build connections that matter

11) **The LinkedIn Code**: Unlock The Largest Online Business Social Network To Get Leads, Prospects & Clients for B2B, Professional Services and Sales & Marketing Pros

12) **LinkedIn For Dummies**

13**) LinkedIn: LinkedIn For Business** - How To Generate More Leads, Build A Relationship With Your Clients And Significantly Increase Your Sales! (LinkedIn Success, LinkedIn Riches, LinkedIn Marketing)

14) **LinkedIn: 21 Top Strategies To Attract Recruiters**, Employers and Networking Your Way To The Job Of Your Dreams! (Social Media Marketing, LinkedIn, Networking, Recruiting, Job Success)

15) **LinkedIn: How To Build A Professional LinkedIn Profile** To Make You Stand Out, Attract Recruiters And Get Your Dream Job! (Career Search, Job Hunting, LinkedIn Makeover)

16) **The Power Formula for LinkedIn Success** (Second Edition - Entirely Revised) : Kick-start Your Business, Brand, and Job Search

17) **How To Build the ULTIMATE LinkedIn Profile In Under An Hour:** Boost Your Branding, Attract Recruiters, And Find Your Next Job

18) **Ultimate Guide to LinkedIn for Business** (Ultimate Series)

19) **LinkedIn (eReport): Use Your Profile To Attract Employers** (e-Report Book 2)

20) **LinkedIn: Profiles That Don't Suck!** Learn the insider LinkedIn success tactics that will have recruiters calling you! (LinkedIn Success, job hunting online, ... career change, jobs search Book 1)

This page intentionally left blank.

RECOMMENDED WEBSITES FOR FURTHER REVIEW

Web: Log an issue/give feedback to LinkedIn - https://help.linkedin.com/app/ask

Web: LinkedIn Investor Relations - http://investors.linkedin.com/

Web: LinkedIn Learning Webinars - https://help.linkedin.com/app/answers/detail/a_id/530

Web: Android History: https://www.android.com/history/

Web: LinkedIn Recruiter Search Result Discrepancies Explored: http://bit.ly/1JCZhrx

Web: Advanced LinkedIn Strategies: http://www.linkedinsights.com/

Web: Customize Your Invitations on the LinkedIn App: http://linkd.in/1FIkpkK

Web: LinkedIn Elevate on the Apple Store: http://apple.co/1Q1FZAl

Web: Become a LinkedIn Search Ninja: https://youtu.be/5-O4R-rvvNk

Web: LinkedIn Mobile Recruiter App: https://www.youtube.com/watch?v=mHl3wH-4moA&feature=youtu.be&t=120

Web: Introducing the New LinkedIn Pulse: Your Daily News, Powered By Your Professional World: http://bit.ly/1KZ4dMu

Web: LinkedIn Member Dashboard Metrics: http://linkd.in/12HhcQN

This page intentionally left blank.

OTHER BOOKS BY THE AUTHOR

LinkedIn Secrets Revealed: 10 Secrets To Unlocking Your
Complete Profile on LinkedIn.com -
http://amzn.to/12pyCNu

Publishing a Book on Amazon: 7 Steps to Publishing your #1 Book
on Amazon Kindle in Minutes!
http://amzn.to/18i9JI3

Build Your Own Living Revocable Trust: A Pocket Guide to
Creating a Living Revocable Trust
http://amzn.to/1CoNUmn

Spirituality in the Workplace: A Study Guide for Business Leaders

http://amzn.to/1CoNUmn

Trapped in a Meritocracy: Cracking the Meritocracy Code: Get Paid More for Valued Performance

http://amzn.to/1zbufrW

Amazon Secrets Revealed: How To Sell More Books on Amazon.com

http://amzn.to/1EBhY1O

Email Inbox Management: How to Master Your Inbox with
Etiquette
http://amzn.to/1JeKK8T

Love or Hate Email... 21 Rules to Change Your - I Must Check my
Email Habit. Get Back to Work and Make Money Again!
http://bit.ly/Love_Email

Note: Most of these links are to Amazon.com eBooks. You can change the sales region, by changing .com to .co.uk etc.

This page intentionally left blank.

QUESTIONS OR COMMENTS?

Do you Need to ask me a question and get an instant response? Email me @ <u>LinkedInSecretsRevealed@gmail.com</u>

I read and answer all emails sent to me, myself! I do not outsource, or crowd source this task!

This page intentionally left blank.

EASTER EGG FUN

Let's pretend it's Easter for a moment!

If you bought this book at a **Half Price Books Store** in Austin, Cedar Park, or Round Rock, Texas I will personally send you a kindle copy of two other titles I have published.

Just email me a copy of your receipt with Subject: Easter Egg & PIMP YOUR PROFILE BOOK PURCHASE.

That's all I need.

Check-out Half Price Books Stores here: http://www.hpb.com/

Again, please email me your receipt @ LinkedInSecretsRevealed@gmail.com

If you got this far in the paperback you might like to know you can get the digital version of this book as well for a **HUGE discount!**

It's called *Kindle Matchbook* and as long as you have made the original purchase on **Amazon.com** you should be able to get the digital ebook for less than a dollar (before tax).

www.ingramcontent.com/pod-product-compliance
Lightning Source LLC
Chambersburg PA
CBHW070832180526
45168CB00002B/810